I'm Drowning in Dreams of the End Times

by

Karen Rivers - Johnson

Dedication

To my Lord and Savior Jesus Christ, I give You thanks for all You've done for me. I thank You for trusting and choosing me in this season to write this book. Thank You for thinking so highly of me that You would give me the courage to step forth and complete such a great assignment. I didn't think I could do it, but I found out that I can be confident in knowing that if You release it into my care, You will anoint, empower and enable me to accomplish the task. And for that, I give You praise.

To my husband, Timothy D. Johnson who has encouraged and covered me throughout this time. Thanks for all your love and support. You will never really know how much I appreciate you because there are no words that could ever express it.

To my three children Rapheal, Montreal and Tanji, and my favorite and only grandson, Cameron; just know that it has been a pleasure being a parent to you all. My heart's desire is that you all will always live a life after Christ and will fulfill your dreams in the process. Always accept the leading of the Holy Spirit and in all that you do.

Acknowledgment

I would like to thank my siblings, Jackie, Deborah, Yvonne, and Robin, for allowing me to preach to them all on many phone and FaceTime calls.

I want to give a Special Acknowledgement to my mentors, Prophetess Tricia Gibson, and Pastor Kim Burrell. Each of them has been rocks for me at different times. You have all given me the strength to continue to pursue God and what He has called me to do. Thanks for helping me cultivate the gifts that are within me. I appreciate you all for never being too busy to hear my little voice on the other end of your phone line. I love you all so much.

Thanks to all of my spiritual siblings, Dr. Rachel Ellis, Evangelists Kathy Burrell, Karen Jordan, Pamela Hutchinson, Prophetess Natasha Kelson, Prophet El Robinson, Pastor James Miller and Prophet Omega George for all of the prayers and encouraging words you have spoken into my life during this time. Thanks to Pastor Benjamin Ellis, Prophetess Dewonna Beck, Prophetess Michelle Page, Apostle Denise Offor, Prophetess Sandra Conway, Prophetess Karen Conway, and Pastor Geraldine Stanford. Thank you for every prophetic word you have ever spoken over me that has catapulted me into my next level in God and business.

Sarah Johnson who I call Momma Sarah I want to thank you for constantly encouraging me to press on when I really wanted to quit. From the day I told you my Mom had passed away and you told me you would be Mom to me, I can truly say you have been nothing less of that, and for this, I say Thanks.

Finally, I give a big thank you to the Sisters of Zion, who continually pray for me and support me by calling in every Saturday morning at 9am ready to travail for the nation and the people of God. I pray your dreams will be fulfilled in this season.

Foreword

We are living in the manifestation of prophecy spoken to us in scripture of old. It is speaking loudly, giving warnings to all of humanity of that great and terrible day of the LORD.

GOD consecrated specific individuals to be a trumpet and to have the discernment of the Spirit of God to be able to point to the work of The Almighty. Prophetess Karen Rivers Johnson is one of those last hour individuals. She is committed to hearing the voice of GOD through an aggressive prayer life and fasting to make herself available as a yielded vessel for GOD.

She is a woman of integrity, a committed wife and mother. She is also a faithful servant at The Mega Life Church. She has a love for people and a desire to lead men and women to Jesus Christ.

I know beyond a shadow of a doubt that the words she speaks are from the mouth of God. Any message given through God's vessel to his people is necessary for the body of Christ. "He that hath an ear let him hear." (Revelation 2:29)

This book will bring to understanding the mysteries of the end-times prophecies. Many scholars may have misjudged the fullness of prophecies in the scriptures by finalizing a prophetic word based upon one event in history. Prophetess Karen Rivers-Johnson understands that prophecy many times has an echoing effect. You may see the same prophecy reoccurring with a louder voice for the same type of people of scripture generations later.

This book will sharpen your understanding of biblical prophecy, as well as strengthen your joy for the completion of your long-awaited salvation.

Pastor Benjamin Ellis

Table of Contents

Introduction

What are dreams? A dream is a succession of images, ideas, emotions and sensations that usually occur involuntarily in the mind during certain states of sleep. (Wikipedia)

Dreaming, in the Bible can be interpreted as God speaking to you. Psalm 12:6 states that God will speak in dreams and visions.

Acts 2:17 reads thus; "And in the last days it shall be God declares, that I will out my Spirit on all flesh, and your sons and your daughters shall prophesy and your young men shall see visions, and your old men shall dream dreams".

According to Job 33:14-18; "For God speaks in one way and in two, though man does not perceive it. In a dream, in a vision of the when deep sleep falls on men, while they slumber on their beds, then he opens the ears of men and terrifies them with warnings, that he may turn man aside from his deed and conceal pride from a man; he keeps back his soul from the pit, his life from perishing by the sword".

Dreams are necessary, especially in this season. God has been gifting so many people with the gift of dreams, visions and interpretation of dreams because of the need to know His exact directions and instructions.

"And as it was in the days of Noah, so shall it be also in the days of the Son of man. They did eat, they drank, they married wives, they were given in marriage, until the day that Noah entered into the ark, and flood came and destroyed them all. Likewise, also as it was in the days of Lot; they die eat, they drank, they bought, they sold, they planted, they builded; But the same day that Lot went out of Sodom it rained fire and brimstone from heaven, and destroyed them all. Even thus shall it be in the day when the Son of Man shall be revealed" (Luke 17:26-30 KJV).

In 2019, God began to give me visions and dreams of the End Times. He revealed to me what to expect and how to warn the people about what was to come. He gave me dreams of the Anti-Christ, his age during this time, and how close we are to his stepping out of hiding. God has even spoken about how near we are to the seven years of tribulation. In this book, I will give you dreams and Interpretations of not only my dreams but dreams from others God has been speaking to concerning the End Times.

The one thing I pray and hope is that this book will encourage you to prepare for the coming of our Lord and Savior, Jesus Christ. He died on the cross over 2000 years ago, and He paid the ransom for us so we wouldn't have to.

Will you open up your heart to receive what God is saying in this hour? Please don't wait any longer, give your life to Him today.

Prayer

"For God so loved the world that He gave His one and only Son, Jesus Christ, that whoever believes in Him shall not perish, but have eternal life". John 3:16

Father God in heaven, I know that I am a sinner and that I need Your forgiveness. I believe in my heart and confess with my mouth that Jesus Christ Is the Son of the Living God.   I believe that He died on the cross for my sins and that You raised Him from the dead. I believe that He is sitting on Your right hand, and He is interceding for me even now. I will trust Him and follow Him from this day forward. I need You to guide me, direct and help me to do Your will.

Today by faith, I believe that I am saved in Jesus name. Amen.

<u>**Chapter One**</u>

DREAM OF SALVATION

I will start off with the dream God gave me shortly after my brother Michael passed away:

In the dream, I walk into a bathroom at my Sister Yvonne's home and I see my brother Michael (who at this time had just passed away). He was sitting in a chair in front of a large mirror. His body appeared transparent, like a water-like solution without a real form, but somehow, I knew it was him. I could somewhat see the form of his body but I could also see through it. He was crying and I asked him what was wrong. He said,

"Do you see what they have done to me? Look at my back".

And on his back were big scars, and I asked him "who did this to you," while crying and weeping. And he just kept crying and never said anything else. Then I heard this song playing in my head, and these were the words of the song:

"When I see my life is broken

It appears to be no hope

I was torn, scorned and abused

But my life has just begun

Can I count on you to love me?

I sit here looking in the mirror

I see clearly through myself

The scars, the hurt, the pain

Wondering what my life would gain

Can I count on you to love me?

Then I heard this as if it was responding to the first verse:

Now when I see My body's broken

And the nail prints in my hand

I was beaten, spit on and misused

By some folk who didn't care

Can I count on you to love Me?

I stand here looking in the mirror

I see stripes laid on My back

I was crucified for your sins

So, you can win in every attack

Can I count on you to love Me? "

As soon as I woke up, I realized that this was a dream about accepting Christ Jesus as your Lord and Savior. The Lord wants us to know, He understands all that we have gone through. But we have to remember all that He went through for us. *This was* to fulfill what was spoken through Isaiah the prophet:

"He Himself took our infirmities and carried away our diseases." (Matthew 8:17)

It is time for us all to prepare for the coming of the Lord. Many things are happening in the Earth to take our focus off of what God is doing in the Earth, and what satan is doing in the Earth. This book I pray will help open your eyes and enlighten you on what is literally going on.

<u>**Chapter Two**</u>

Walk-in Your Assignment, you know the one you gave up on.

"Let the wind of God breath again over your ministry. Breath again over your dreams. Breath again in your business. If you had the faith to birth it, then you can have the faith to carry it through until God says it's over. Have the faith to walk it out and take one step at a time if that is what it takes."

This was a Prophetic Word given to me in August of 2018 by Bishop Tonya Kearney. The Lord came to me and spoke in August 2018 and said to me,

"Restart Sisters of Zion Prayer Ministry."

I said to the Lord, "if this is You Lord, give me a confirmation."

You know when we don't really want to do something, we always need confirmation. Well, two days later, I attended a Women's Conference that was hosted by Bishop Tonya Kearney and she walked up to me after the service was over and said,

"May I pray for you?"

Not knowing her in the natural but in the Spirit, I said "yes". She said to me,

"God gave you a Ministry and you gave It to someone else that didn't care for it. God said this time you birth this Ministry, hold on to it, and don't let it go."

When I returned home after the Conference, The Lord said

"Go to Ezekiel 37:1-10 and read it."

So, I read the verses and God said to me, "Can your Ministry live again?"

There are many of us who, at one time or another, God gave a ministry to, a ministry that was connected to our destiny, but we decided to give it up for whatever reason.

Whether it was a Ministry to the Elderly in the nursing homes, or starting a youth neighborhood Bible study. God wanted us to start it and continue in it to fulfill His Agenda.

I want to talk to those who can relate to this, whether you gave up your Ministry or you allowed it to die. I was one of those young women who was afraid to step out on what God called me to do. Even when I eventually stepped out into the water, I allowed the enemy to convince me that I wasn't enough. I was actually afraid to continue the Prayer Ministry God had given me. After 3 years, I handed the Ministry over to someone I thought was better qualified to lead it than I was. But only after just a few months she let the ministry die, and Sisters of Zion was no more.

Now 20 years later, in 2018, I hear the Lord say

"Do it again, begin again, but this time after you birth this ministry, hold on to it, and don't let go."

So, I am 1.5 years into being obedient to The Lord. Once I decided to be obedient to God, He began to assign me to do other assignments. Well, writing this book on The End Times is one of them, and I am excited about it but yet still a little fearful. The Lord spoke to me this early morning and said, "The enemy wants us to live in fear because he fears us. He fears who we are and what we can do".

With Obedience to God, comes blessings, and that is what I have experienced over the past 7 months and want to continue to experience. I can't even tell you how blessed I have become, and what kind of doors the Lord has opened for my husband and me. (Isaiah 1:18, "If you consent and obey, you will eat the best of the land)

So, today, I encourage you to complete the task that God has assigned to you. Don't wait for someone else to do it. You were God's first choice, but if you decide not to, someone else will be His choice. And with their obedience, they shall eat the best of the land. Don't you want to have all that God wants to give you before Jesus returns? I know I do, so just decide today to give God what He wants, and He will give you what you desire.

Chapter Three

The 7 Churches, where do you stand?

The 7 Churches in Revelation received spiritual directions from God through Jesus Christ after evaluating each of them separately.

Revelation's first and second chapters will be discussed in this chapter.

The Church of Ephesus is found in Turkey. Turkey is positioned 95% in Asia and only 5% in Europe. For some reason, many of us thought that Ephesus or Turkey was in Europe.

Revelation 1:4b-5 reads

But I have this against you, that you have left your first love. Therefore, remember from where you have fallen, and repent and do the deeds you did at first; or else I am coming to you and will remove your lampstand out of its place—unless you repent.

This word was to the Asians, and China covers a majority a part of that continent. The one thing that I know is that, if you dream of Asians, they represent being smart and intelligent. They depend on their own intelligence to guide and direct them. So, when the Word says, "you have left your first love", it's partially talking about them loving and trusting in themselves and their own minds. Also, they have now left the only true God to worship other gods like buddha. This scripture shows at one time God was pleased with them. My Prayer is that they return to the one and only True God, Jehovah God, Jesus our Savior and Lord.

Verse 7 reads, "To him who overcomes, I will grant to eat of the tree of life which is in the Paradise of God".

God is telling them if they can overcome this, they will be granted a place in God's Paradise. If not He will remove their candle from the lampstand. What they must overcome is the lust to serve and trust in themselves and other gods.

The Second Church is the church of Smyrna, which is also in Asia.

Revelation 1:9-10

"I know your tribulation and your poverty (but you are rich), and the blasphemy by those who say they are Jews and are not, but are a synagogue of Satan. Do not fear what you are about to suffer. Behold, the devil is about to cast some of you into prison, so that you will be tested, and you will have tribulation for ten days."

It seems that the Lord was not disappointed in the Smyrna church, because they were doing what was right in his. However, they are being warned that they are going to suffer some persecution. The Lord said to them,

"Be faithful until death, and I will give you the crown of life.

The third church is Pergamum, which is the today, Bergama, Turkey. It is said that all that is left of the city of Pergamum, are ruins. When the Apostle John wrote his letter to the Pergamum church, it was one of the most influential cities in the Roman Empire. The people of Pergamum were inventors and innovators. Antipas a Man of God, was killed here because he refused to worship the Roman gods. According to the scriptures in Revelation 2:12-15

"The One who has the sharp two-edged sword says this:

'I know where you dwell, where Satan's throne is; and you hold fast My name, and did not deny My faith even in the days of Antipas, My witness, My faithful one, who was killed among you, where Satan dwells. But I have a few things against you, because you have there some who hold the teaching of Balaam, who kept teaching Balak to put a stumbling block before the sons of Israel, to eat things sacrificed to idols and to commit acts of immorality."

After His evaluation of Pergamum He then says in Revelation 2:17

"To him who overcomes, to him I will give some of the hidden manna, and I will give him a white stone, and a new name written on the stone which no one knows but he who receives it." It appears that there were yet some who continued in the Faith. So those who God was pleased with were offered gifts that no one else had or even knew about.

Thyatira, the fourth church of the seven, is now the modern Turkish city of Akhisar or may be called Lydian. It lies in the far west of Turkey, south of Istanbul and almost east of Athens. Thyatira means hill graveyard. They were a prosperous trading town that was located on the Roman road from Pergamos to Laodicea.

"I know your deeds, and your love and faith and service and perseverance, and that your deeds of late are greater than at first. But I have this against you, that you tolerate the woman Jezebel, who calls herself a prophetess, and she teaches and leads My bond-servants astray so that they commit acts of immorality and eat things sacrificed to idols." Revelation 2:19-20

God was not pleased with his church in Thyatira for allowing the woman, Jezebel, to teach false doctrine to believers (Revelation 2:20-23).

The real-life Jezebel was the wife of King Ahab, who was considered to be the worst king of Israel in the Bible days. With what God has shown me in dreams, the spirit of Jezebel will show up again very soon in the End Times, which I will talk about later on in the book.

The Church of Sardis, the fifth of the seven churches is located in Manisa province in western Turkey.

There was a disaster that came to the city in 17 AD, where Sardis was destroyed by an earthquake. And then It was rebuilt with the help of many, who were exempt from paying taxes for five years history explains.

Revelation 3:1-6

"He who has the seven Spirits of God and the seven stars, says this: 'I know your deeds, that you have a name that you are alive, but you are dead. Wake up, and strengthen the things that remain, which were about to die; for I have not found your deeds completed in the sight of My God. So, remember what you have received and heard; and keep it, and repent. Therefore, if you do not wake up, I will come like a thief, and you will not know at what hour I will come to you.

But you have a few people in Sardis who have not soiled their garments; and they will walk with Me in white, for they are worthy. He who overcomes will thus be clothed in white garments; and I will not erase his name from the book of life, and I will confess his name before My Father and before His angels. He who has an ear, let him hear what the Spirit says to the churches."

The church at Sardis had a number of faults, although some were faithful. They were spiritually dead overall, despite having a reputation of being spiritually alive (Revelation 3:2). Jesus's evaluation of Sardis shows they were lacking many good qualities, regardless of doing good works (verse 3).

Those in Sardis desperately needed to spiritually wake up and repent. Having the knowledge of the truth, they still refused to practice it.

The great thing is that there were still some who were faithful and walked with Christ. Because of that, their names would not be removed from the book of life and the Lord will acknowledge them before the Father.

The majority of the people at Sardis were spiritually weak, much like the members of the Laodicean church later described in the same chapter. There were very few who were committed and converted Christians.

Tradition states that Sardis was the first in its area to be converted by the preaching of the apostle John.

The Church of Philadelphia the sixth out of the seven churches which is located in the district of Manisa Province in the Aegean region of Turkey.

Revelation 3:8-13

"He who is holy, who is true, who has the key of David, who opens and no one will shut, and who shuts and no one opens, says this:

I know your deeds. Behold, I have put before you an open door which no one can shut, because you have a little power, and have kept My word, and have not denied My name. Behold, I will cause those of the synagogue of Satan, who say that they are Jews and are not, but lie—I will make them come and bow down at your feet, and make them know that I have loved you. Because you have kept the word of My perseverance, I also will keep you from the hour of testing, that hour which is about to come upon the whole world, to test those who dwell on the earth. I am coming quickly; hold fast what you have, so that no one will take your crown. He who overcomes, I will make him a pillar in the temple of My God, and he will not go out from it anymore; and I will write on him the name of My God, and the name of the city of My God, the new Jerusalem, which comes down out of heaven from My God, and My new name. He who has an ear, let him hear what the Spirit says to the churches."

The city was nearly destroyed and suffered a great deal when a major earthquake hit the area in 17 A.D. Because of the devastation, the people of Philidelphia were able to live without paying taxes. This was one Church that God was totally pleased with.

The Church of Laodicea was the seventh of the seven churches, which is now situated near the modern city of Denizli, Turkey. The definition of Laodicean is lukewarm or indifferent in religion or politics.

Laodicea, like Rome, Jerusalem and several other cities, was built upon seven hills. It prospered primarily due to its trade route location, which made it a hub for large money transactions.

The sheep there were known for their fine black wool. The city had many inscriptions showing evidence that they worshiped the pagan deity Zeus.

Laodicea often suffered from earthquakes. It was completely destroyed when an earthquake occurred during the reign of Emperor Nero. The inhabitants were so wealthy that they declined Roman assistance to rebuild the city and instead opted to quickly rebuild it at their own expense.

Revelation 3:14-21 reads, the Amen, the faithful and true Witness, the Beginning of the creation of God, says this:

"I know your deeds, that you are neither cold nor hot; I wish that you were cold or hot. So, because you are lukewarm, and neither hot nor cold, I will spit you out of My mouth. Because you say, "I am rich, and have become wealthy, and have need of nothing," and you do not know that you are wretched and miserable and poor and blind and naked, I advise you to buy from Me gold refined by fire so that you may become rich, and white garments so that you may clothe yourself, and that the shame of your nakedness will not be revealed; and eye salve to anoint your eyes so that you may see. Those whom I love, I reprove and discipline; therefore, be zealous and repent. Behold, I stand at the door and knock; if anyone hears My voice and opens the door, I will come in to him and will dine with him, and he with Me. He who overcomes, I will grant to him to sit down with Me on My throne, as I also overcame and sat down with My Father on His throne."

While reading this chapter on the Seven Churches, can you see which church Jesus would place your name in? Will you be named among those who Jesus would spit out of His mouth or would you be among those who the Lord says, "Well done thy good and faithful servant? This is the time do ask yourself these questions." Don't wait until the Lord returns and you then began to question where you stand in Christ.

Chapter Four

All These Are the Beginning of Sorrows

Matthew 24

And as He sat upon the mount of Olives, the disciples came unto Him privately, saying, tell us when shall these things be? And what shall be the sign of thy coming and of the end of the world? And Jesus answered and said unto them, take heed that no man deceive you. For many shall come in My name, saying, I am Christ; and shall deceive many. And ye shall hear of wars and rumors of wars; see that ye be not troubled: for all these things must come to pass, but the end is not yet. For nation shall rise against nation, and kingdom against kingdom; and there shall be famines, and pestilences, and earthquakes, in divers' places. All these are the beginning of sorrows. verses 3-8

Revelation 6:7-8 reads

And when he had opened the fourth seal, I heard the voice of the fourth beast say, come and see. And I looked, and behold a pale horse; and his name that sat on him was Death, and Hell followed with him. And power was given unto them over the fourth part of the earth, to kill with sword, and with hunger, and with death, and with the beasts of the earth.

Revelation 9:14-15

Saying to the sixth angel which had the trumpet, Loose the four angels which are bound in the great river Euphrates.

And the four angels were loosed, which were prepared for an hour, and a day and a month and a year, for to slay the third part of men. And the number of the army of the horsemen were two hundred thousand thousand; and I heard the number of them. And thus, I saw the horses in the vision, and them that sat on them, having breastplates of fire; red and of jacinth; blue and brimstone; yellow and the heads of the horses were as the heads of lions; and out of their mouths issued fire and smoke and brimstone.

In the Hebrew Year of 5780, which is 2020 for us who are American and not Jewish, the meaning of the year 2020 is to widen your mouth in Wisdom. This year is not about 20/20 vision it's about what comes out of our mouth. What are you speaking? Are you speaking death or life? Are you speaking Truths or facts?

In the 24th chapter of Matthew, Christ is giving us what signs we can look for in order to know His coming is near. He said we shall hear of wars and rumors of wars. For nation shall rise against nation and kingdom against kingdom. And there shall be famines and pestilence, and earthquakes in different places. So, when these things come to pass, we then will know that this is just the beginning of sorrows.

Revelation 6:7-8 bears witness of Matthew 24. I will discuss Revelation 6:7-8 in relation to a dream the Lord gave me on January 20, 2020.

First let me give you the timeline of the Coronavirus per New York Times.

December 31, 2019, the government of Wuhan, China confirmed that they were treating dozens of cases.

January 11, 2020 the Chinese reported the first known death from the Coronavirus.

January 20, 2020 the first confirmed cases outside of China occurred in Korea, Japan, and Thailand. The first confirmed case in the U.S. was reported the very next day in Washington State, where a man in his 30's developed symptoms after returning from a trip to Wuhan, China.

I had a dream on January 20, 2020 that I, my three younger Sisters and our families were out in the country living in a cave-like home we had built. We were just about to celebrate my grandson's birthday it appeared. I saw the date of January 21, 2020 hanging up in the Cave over the party table. This was very odd to me because January 21st is actually my sister, Deborah's birthday, not Cameron's.

Cameron's birthday is in November.

Suddenly in the dream, I saw four warplanes from four different countries flying over our head. One plane was red, one blue, one yellow, and one grayish black. My entire family ran into the cave to hide from the planes because we were not sure what was going on. I do remember that there were people from my Sisters of Zion Prayer Group there in the cave with us. I could see from the front area of the cave that there were thousands of Black Americans across the street from us that were partying and having fun on their land, even when they saw the warplanes flying over their heads.

Then the planes starting flying really low over the people heads who were outside partying. Huge rocks started falling from the planes. The rocks looked like a red, raspberry color powder. The planes began to throw the large rocks of powder onto the wall of their homes, cars and everything that was on their land. Then there was a plane that started dropping gigantic rocks that were so big that when they hit the ground, it caused giant holes to form. Then the plane dropped one large rock in the front of our cave and it made a big black muddy hole, which started bubbling up on our land but it never flowed over onto the land. I saw a gold piece of fabric wrap around that hole but it never touched the inside of the hole. After the planes flew off, I noticed that many of the children across the street were fighting while so many of the others had fallen dead from the powder that was dropped on them. Then I woke up.

The interpretation of this dream is found partially in Daniel 12:1-4, Matthew 24:3-8, Revelation 6:7-8, and Revelation 9:14-15.

I believe that part of this dream speaks of the Coronavirus. Let me show you why.

I had the dream on January 20, 2020, and I saw the date of January 21, 2020. On January 20, 2020 the first case of the Coronavirus was confirmed outside of China. On January 21, 2020 the U.S. had its first confirmed case recorded in Washington State.

In my dream we were about to celebrate my grandson's birthday but his birthday is in November. The first confirmed case in Wuhan, China was in November 2019 posted by the South China Morning Post News. Are all these coincidences? I think not. Now let's look at the powdery substance that was being dropped from the warplanes on the Black Americans.

The Washington Post records that in Wisconsin 73% of the Coronavirus death cases were Black Americans. In Chicago 67% of the cases were Black Americans. Louisiana has a high rate of 70% and Washington D.C. has a percentage of 58% of Black American deaths due to the

Coronavirus. This dream is no coincidence, God was trying to show me something.

Let's continue the interpretation of the dream. The mud hole that was covered with the gold fabric represented those who were preserved in Christ for the Resurrection. The Black Americans that were fighting against one another represents those who have taken the mark of the beast contending with those who had not. The four planes represent the four kingdoms of the antichrist that are coming to destroy the people of God. My family and my Prayer group represents the body of Christ here on Earth. The four planes also represent the four horsemen of the Apocalypse.

The planes in my dream were red, blue, yellow and gray. Look how Revelation 9:15 speaks of the horsemen having on breastplates of fire (red), jacinth (blue), brimstone (yellow), and it said smoke was coming out of its mouth (gray). The cave we were hiding in which was our home, represents the secret place of God, just like Elijah hid in the cave and relied on God to pour out His Spirit on him.

Some warning dreams give us an ample amount of time to prepare for what is to come. However, I believe God had already sent warnings to us before He began to give me this dream. I will show you why I believe this, as we walk through this book of dreams.

Even though we are in these last days and the enemy has turned up the fire against us, we still have a voice to cry out unto our God, and Jesus said He will answer. The one thing the Lord told me to write in this book was, whenever the time comes where we are trapped in our homes and we are unable to come together as a church in a building, He said remember the times the Jews Worshiped, Praised and Prayed to God. Those times are 6am, 9am, 12pm, 3pm, 6pm, and 9pm, the Lord said use these times to Worship, Praise and Pray to Me and you all will still be in one accord and I will heal the land.

<u>CHAPTER Five</u>

Where Is Your Focus?

On January 23, 2020, my sister, Deborah had a dream that she and I were on the beach and the water was a beautiful dark blue color. We were standing inside of a white building on the beach. After gazing and admiring how beautiful the scenery was, we decided to walk outside and get some Sun. After walking outside, we looked up into the sky and we saw a blanket of large stones that looked like boulders were hanging in the sky as if they were waiting to fall like rain upon the Earth. We immediately rushed back into the building. Then we noticed that all of the people of the Jewish descendants that were living in America were packing up and leaving. She said she could hear some saying

"We are leaving this place, because America is about to be destroyed."

Then she woke up from the dream.

Interpretation of this dream is:

We are blood Sisters and we represent Christian sisters around the World. The beach represents Communion with God, and Revelation from God. The sand on the beach represents the good thoughts that God communicates to us about ourselves. The beautiful dark blue water represents the Power of the Holy Spirit. This dream was showing us that we need to prepare for an attack on America, on those who are focused on freedom, and those who focus on the freedom to do the work of God. Because we are black women, in this dream the color black represents those who are aware of God's mysteries. The mystery or revelation here was that we need to escape the judgment which was about to happen because the rocks represented Judgement.

On January 23, 2020 the New York Times reported that Wuhan, with more than eleven million people, were cut off by the Chinese authorities. Because of the Coronavirus they canceled planes, trains, buses, subways and ferries, where none were able to come in or go out.

Matthew 24:7-8 says

For nation shall rise against nation, and kingdom against kingdom: and there shall be famines, and pestilences, and earthquakes, in divers' places. All these are the beginning of sorrows.

The Coronavirus is nothing but a pestilence that has been allowed to enter the Earth by God. Yes, it is probably man-made; however, God allowed it to enter into the Earth because of our disobedience to Him.

Per OXFAM International, Today, the world stands on the brink of unprecedented famines. It states that 30 million people are experiencing alarming hunger, severe levels of food insecurity and malnutrition in Northeastern Nigeria, South Sudan, Somalia, and Yemen.

According to Feeding America, more than 38 million people are living in poverty right here in America. More than 38 million people in the United States struggle with hunger, and 11 million of them being children.

As I write this information, I find myself weeping and my heart aching, because we who are considered one of the richest countries in the world still have more than 11 million children hungry daily. There is famine in divers places throughout the Earth.

On April 21, 2020 reported by USGS, there were more than 56 Earthquakes so far this year from the U.S. to Indonesia, China, Japan, Burma, Honduras, Russia, Croatia, Turkey and many others.

The Bible says when we see these things happening, then know that we are in the beginning of sorrows. We cannot deny that we are drawing near the end times.

This is not the time to slip back into sin, or to walk away from God. This is not the time to listen to those who say "there is no God, or Jesus isn't Lord." However, it is the time to Repent, and witness to all who you come in contact with. Tell them about our wonderful Savior, Jesus Christ and what He did for us over 2000 years ago.

CHAPTER Six

Warning to All Leaders

Revelation 5:5

I saw in the right hand of Him who sat on the throne a book written inside and on the back, sealed up with seven seals. And I saw a strong angel proclaiming with a loud voice, "Who is worthy to open the book and to break its seals?" And no one in heaven or on the earth or under the earth was able to open the book or to look into it. Then I began to weep greatly because no one was found worthy to open the book or to look into it; and one of the elders said to me, "Stop weeping; behold, the Lion that is from the tribe of Judah, the Root of David, has overcome so as to open the book and its seven seals."

My husband, Timothy had a warning dream for the spiritual leaders around the world. During this time, we were under a great, no nonsense Leader, Pastor Kim Burrell when Tim had this dream. The dream started with everyone sitting in the Sanctuary waiting for service to begin. However, it appeared to be more like it was going to be a meeting instead of a normal service. He noticed that all ministers had on their clergy attire in this particular service. The doors that she usually walks through to enter into the Sanctuary swung open.

When Pastor Kim walked in, she was wearing a long purple robe, and in her right hand was a long golden sword, and in the left hand she had her Bible and a Scroll in her hand.

In front of her was a giant Lion walking into the Sanctuary. He entered the pulpit before her, sat down, and began to scan the room. Pastor Kim then stepped into the pulpit, took the sword and planted it into the stage, and then opened the scroll. When she opened the scroll, she began to read off the names, and after each name that was called out, the Lion roared. When the Lion roared it was a signal to let the person whose name was called know to get up and leave out of the Sanctuary. After about 6 names that were called out, Tim woke up from the dream.

Here is the interpretation to the dream:

The Lion represents the Lion of Judah, and the church in the dream represents the entire Body of Christ. The Lord was speaking to Tim about what He is doing in this hour concerning the whole Body of Christ here on Earth.

The first thing we are going to see is that it's time for the Lion of Judah to step on the scene. Jesus is going to bring some hard things to our attention from the pulpit.

The next thing we are going to see is, Judgement from the Lord. Pastor Kim in this dream, represents the Pastor of the entire Body of Christ. Whenever we dream about a Pastor whether male or female, they usually represent the Lord. We know that in this dream she represents the Lord because of the Golden Sword she is carrying into the Sanctuary, which is the Sword of the Spirit, or the Sword of the Lord. (Hebrews 4:12, For the Word of God is quick and powerful, and sharper than any two-edged sword piercing even to the dividing asunder of soul and spirit, and of the joints and marrow and is a discerner of the thoughts and intents of the heart).

The scroll represents the book which our names are written in. The Lord is going to judge the leaders of His church. When He calls their name and if they have not been listening to what He has said for them to do, they are going to have to get up and leave. Which means they are either going to retire, or they going to die. The time of judgement is at hand.

This is one of the dreams God had given before the Coronavirus, to warn His people of the judgement which was just ahead.

November 4, 2019 the Lord gave me a vision. I saw a Lion sitting up and looking from right to left while a little lamb sat next to Him. It seemed like He was protecting the lamb.

The interpretation of this dream shows that God is going to reveal Himself not only as the Lamb of God but also the Lion of the tribe of Judah, the Conqueror, and the Victor. The Lion and the Lamb represents the end times.

<u>CHAPTER Seven</u>

The Disasters in the Land

Amos 3:7-8 "Surely the Lord God does nothing unless He reveals His secret counsel to His servants the prophets. The Lion has roared, Who will not fear? The Lord God has spoken, Who can but prophesy?"

The Lord is speaking of the leaders, especially the prophets who are giving instructions by the leading of the Holy Spirit.

God has been sending us signs after signs of the last days through His prophets. When we as the body of Christ stopped listening, disasters started coming to the Earth.

According to Wikipedia:

January 12, 2010 there was a 7.0 magnitude earthquake that hit Haiti and allegedly over 220,000 people were killed.

February 27, 2010 just a month later a 8.8 magnitude earthquake hit Chile.

March 2010 a drought came upon 5 southwestern provinces in China.

August 7, 2010 there was a huge mudslide in Gansu Province in China, and more than 1471 people were killed.

September 4, 2010 New Zealand was hit by a 7.2 magnitude earthquake.

January 12, 2011 Australia was flooded.

March 11, 2011 a 9.0 magnitude earthquake hit the East Coast of Japan, creating a giant Tsunami.

In March and April high temperatures in Switzerland and Germany led to many wildfires.

June 2011 there was a volcano eruption in Chile.

Between July 2011 and October 2011 Bangkok Thailand experienced its worst floods in 50 years.

July 2011 till August 2011 East Africa experienced great famines in the land.

July 2012 till August 2012 many states in America experienced record-breaking droughts.

July 2012 Beijing China experienced extreme rainfalls.

October 2012 the U.S. was hit by Sandy a great hurricane. It was the deadliest and most destructive, as well as the strongest hurricane of the 2012 season.

June 2013 India was flooded.

July 2013 a constant haze took over central and eastern China.

August 25, 2013 strong winds caused fires to spiral out of control in California, resulting in its largest wildfire in history.

December 2013 the Middle East was blanketed by its first snow storm in 100 years.

January 2, 2014 a cold wave hit North America which was the U.S. and parts of Canada.

September 27, 2014 a volcano on Mount Ontake Japan erupted killing 63 people.

April 2015 an earthquake struck Nepal, killing 9,000 people and injuring nearly 22,000.

June 2015 a massive flood hit Tbilisi, GA killed at least 12 people and caused animals to be released from city's Zoo into the streets.

January 4, 2016 a 6.8 magnitude earthquake hit Northeast India.

February 6, 2016 an earthquake hit Kaohsiung, Taiwan, causing 116 deaths.

In 2016 Wildfires in California alone costs $990,000,000.

In 2017 Hurricane Harvey alone cost Texas, Louisiana, and Alabama $125,000,000,000.

In 2017 Hurricane Irma cost Florida, South Carolina, GA, and Puerto Rico $64,760,000,000.

2018 Wildfires again in California now costs $16,000,000,000.

2019-2020 an outbreak of desert locusts impacts East Africa.

From December 2019 until today the Coronavirus pandemic is an ongoing pandemic for the entire World. It was first identified in Wuhan China. As of May 2020, allegedly there are 3.68 million cases reported in 185 countries, resulting in over 261,131 deaths, and more than 1.21 million people recovered.

The economic fallout could include recessions in the U.S., euro-area and Japan, the slowest growth on record in China, and a total of cost in the U.S. is over $2 trillion, the European countries have announced their own spending blitz, and Japan has approved a nearly $1 trillion economic stimulus packages, says NY Times.

These disasters alone should open up the eyes of all mankind, helping us to understand that God is speaking to us, and He isn't pleased with what He sees.

As a voice and mouthpiece of God, I pray you will heed to His instructions, and humbly come back to Him in repentance.

CHAPTER Eight

What does the Bible say about dreams?

Job 33:15-18

"For God speaks in one way, and in two, though man does not perceive it. In a dream, in a vision of the night, when deep sleep falls on men, while they slumber on their beds, then he opens the ears of men and terrifies them with warnings, that he may turn man aside from his deed and conceal pride from a man; he keeps back his soul from the pit, his life from perishing by the sword."

God will seal our directions in the night hours through our dreams the Bible says. The Holy Spirit is directing our footsteps through visions.

Psalms 37:23

"The steps of a good man are ordered by the Lord: and he delighted in his way."

So, the directions that God wants to take us in, He will sometimes wait to speak it when we are asleep. There are many of us who don't take the time to sit and wait on the Lord to speak to us in prayer, so, He has to speak to some of us in dreams and visions.

God gives dreams when He wants to turn people from their own direction. God spoke to the wise men, He told them not to go back the same way they came, it was to spare their lives.

Matthew 2:12 "And having being warned by God in a dream not to return to Herod, the Magi left their own country by another way. "

The Lord also spoke to Joseph in a dream, He warned Joseph about Herod killing the babies under 2 years of age. He told him to leave Bethlehem and flee to Egypt to save the baby Jesus's life. Herod heard that a new King of the Jews will arise and he became insecure, so he ordered all babies under 2 years old to be killed.

Matthew2:13

Now when they had gone, behold, an angel of the Lord appeared to Joseph in a dream and said, "Get up? Take the Child and His mother and flee to Egypt, and remain there until I tell you; for Herod is going to search for the Child to destroy Him."

If Joseph had not known the voice of God, and obeyed His voice, the baby Jesus could have been killed. Then God would have had to start over again with another plan. Why? Because God wanted to redeem His children, us, back to Himself.

There is a Jewish belief that God visits the Earth between 3am-6am in the mornings because everything is calm and quiet during this time. This is the time that Jesus usually arose to pray. Many believed that if you happen to be up during this time and in that particular area, God will visit you and give you revelation and an inspired word. This is also the time God gives dreams and visions. I know that whenever God gives me a prophetic dream, it is usually around 4am, the time I am supposed to get up for prayer. It helps me to remember my dreams, so that I am able to write them down. I am so grateful that God even takes the time to speak to little me.

Dreams were given in the Bible days and are now given to us for Warnings, Directions, Wisdom, and Understanding. It can also show you your future. God has frequently made use of dreams in communicating His will to men and women. For instance, look at the history of Jacob, Laban, Joseph, Gideon, and Solomon. God not only gives the dreams but He will give you the interpretation. My favorite of them all is Joseph in Genesis, where God gave the butler and baker a dream and Joseph gave the interpretation. Just as Joseph interpreted it, it happened, which shows us, God is Lord over our dreams.

Whenever you dream, take the time to seek God for the interpretation. It is not always what we think the dream means, remember this is God communicating with us His way. The word says, His ways are not our ways, and His thoughts are not ours.

CHAPTER Nine

2 Chronicles 7:14

"If My People, which are called by My name, shall humble themselves, and pray, and seek My face, and turn from their wicked ways; then will I hear from heaven, and will forgive their sins, and will heal their land. "

This is a promise that the Lord gave us. We are in the last days. I didn't say we are in the days of the great tribulation, but I believe with what God has shown me, we are in the beginning days of sorrow in what the Bible speaks of.

With the pestilence in the land, the Coronavirus, we should be drawn to prayer. We should have the desire to seek the face of God and turn from our wicked ways. But how many of us are really seeking the face of God while we are shut-in?

I remember when I was young, the church would call a shut-in on a Friday night and we wouldn't leave out till Saturday morning after we had breakfast. During the time of us being shut-in, there would be someone that would lead us into prayer for about 30 minutes and then we went for a break. You would hear one person just crying out to God for their children, saying, "save my children God, don't let them go to hell", then from another corner of the church, you would hear someone else praising God for delivering their child from drugs. Someone else in a different corner would be singing a song of worship to God, while someone else would be travailing for their spouse. So, all night you would hear so much going on but it never sounded like chaos, it only sounded like cries to the Father. You could hear faith in their prayers. When morning came, great sounds of rejoicing from all the people would wake the children up, and they would be looking around like, what did I miss.

The praise came from the people of God because they knew God had heard their cry and they could be reassured; change had already begun.

Shut in's in the church were voluntary, but now God has allowed us to be forced into a shut in. While we are here, what are we doing with our time? This is the time we can pray for our children to be saved. Now is the time for us to send up timber for the Body of Christ to come back to their first Love. We can pray without ceasing. Remember what you said to God right before we went into the shut in? Someone was saying, "God, I just wish I could spend more time with You." "Lord, I wish I could take off for two months for vacation just to pray and communion with You." " Father, I am so tired, I just need a little rest." Well God heard your cry, and He answered your prayer. However, are you spending time with Him any more than before? Are you praying and communing with Him daily? Are you getting the necessary rest you so needed? We have to be careful not to miss the answer for something we prayed, because we may never get it again.

Revelation 3:15-16, 19

"I know your deeds, that you are neither cold nor hot; I wish that you were cold or hot. So, because you are lukewarm, and neither hot nor cold, I spit you out of My mouth." "Those whom I love, I reprove and discipline; therefore, be zealous and repent."

This is why the Lord spoke to Bobby Conner and said, "If I can find a people without mixture, I will pour out My power without measure." God wants to endow us with His Power, but He can only pour His Power and Spirit into clean vessels. We can't be straddling the fence and expect God to give us His Power and Anointing. The Bible says that the Holy Spirit cannot dwell in an unclean temple. You can't be saved today, and in the clubs tomorrow. You can't love your co-workers and hate your neighbor. God is looking for a clean vessel He can pour Himself into, to use for His glory, in His Power. Are you willing to repent and become zealous?

Someone who is zealous spends a lot of time or energy in supporting something that they believe in very strongly. (Collins Dictionary). Can God count on you to be supportive of His Word and ways?

The enemy wants to distract us from fulfilling purpose in life. Not only distracting us from fulfilling purpose, but also from seeking the face of God, where He can reveal to us the schemes of the enemy.

On February 28, 2020 I had 3 dreams. When you have several dreams in the same night they are always connected. So, the first dream was that I saw some sort of vision of people standing behind and around this Ouija board. As the Ouija board moved the people were in sync with it moving. Now at the same time, more people were standing about 4 feet away in front of the Ouija board whose body was also in sync with moving with the board. I remember they had no control over their movement, but yet they were okay. with that. I was thinking to myself, aren't they concerned about not having control? All I saw was a lot of laughter coming from them.

Interpretation of this dream is: These two sets of people represents the Body of Christ and all of Mankind. An Ouija board is a board that is used to call upon spirits outside of God and the Holy Spirit to move things and receive answers for questions they have. This dream is about people in the church and outside of the church who are looking for an answer to connect with spirits outside of God. This shows that the enemy is going to start using the body of Christ and they won't even be aware of it. While the enemy will start to use them, they will be laughing, thinking that this is just a game. However, it is not a game, the enemy is making his play in these end times. He will also begin to use people who have given themselves over to other spirits other than the Holy Spirit.

I then dreamed a second dream; I saw a newborn baby of about 2 weeks old holding up a baby that was about 2 months old. The older baby was laying back on the youngest baby. The 2-week-old baby's eyes were closed, but the 2-month-old baby's eyes were wide open.

I could see he had beautiful blue eyes, and they were fixed on something. I was unable to see what he was looking at but I could see him being very attentive and focused on something. He was looking as if something serious was going on.

The interpretation of this dream is: There is something new that has been birth into the world and it's only been around for a very short time. It will lead to the birthing of something else into this world.

The blue represents communion and revelation from God. So, if we can stay focused on communion with God, and receive revelation from Him, then He can reveal to us how to counteract the enemy. He will say "this is what the enemy is doing, but if you focus on communion with Me, and be attentive to My revelation, in just a short time I will birth something new into the Earth for you."

The last dream I had that night was; I saw a gold bowl with 2 handles on the sides and a pink rose pattern on the bowl. The gold bowl was sitting on a table as if it was set up for a foot washing during a communion time.

The interpretation of this dream is; Gold represents God's glory, and the number 2 represents multiplication. The pink rose that I saw on the bowl represents childlike love in God. God is revealing to us that in a very short time this will give birth to God's glory. It will be a reservoir flowing through our lives, with that childlike faith and love from our Father, God. He wants to wash us in His childlike faith, so His glory will flow through us double.

These dreams are to encourage the entire body of Christ that if we would focus on heaven, communing with God and His revelation like that baby was focused, something will be birth into the Earth for His people. If we focus on who He is, how much He loves us and wants to commune with us, there will be a birthing of God's glory, and the ability to receive the child like faith and love from above.

This is the time and season that the enemy is moving his pieces into place. However, God is giving birth to a generation who will focus on Him, so His glory can flow through the land. So again, I ask "Can God count on you to be supportive of His Word and Ways?

<u>CHAPTER Ten</u>

Beware of the Anti-Christ

1 John 2:18-23

Children, it is the last hour; and just as you heard that antichrist is coming, even now many antichrists have appeared; from this we know that it is the last hour. They went out from us, but they were not really of us; for if they had been of us, they would have remained with us; but they went out, so that it would be shown that they all are not of us. But you have an anointing from the Holy One, and you all know. I have not written to you because you do not know the truth, but because you do know it, and because no lie is of the truth. Who is the liar but the one who denies that Jesus is the Christ? This the antichrist, the one who denies the Father and the Son. Whoever denies the Son does not have the Father; the one who confesses the Son has the Father also.

On February 24, 2020, my son, Rapheal had a very interesting dream. He dreamed he was standing on a hilltop, and he saw a hand that was not made of flesh. The hand had a vine growing out of it with a face that could speak. A woman was sitting next to it, and she was talking to it. On one side of her was a floating black rock. The plant and the lady were conversing. Then the lady asked the plant, "are you reading my thoughts?" The plant responded "No", then the lady continued to talk. The plant eyes started glowing red, and the black floating rock began to speak, and it said "don't do it, don't do it" Then there were two images of the lady's face side by side that began to merge into one face. A blue color shadow began to cover the lady's face, and then this strange feeling came over her. She then says to the plant, "Yes, you are reading my thoughts." Then everything began to grow dark around her, and she says "I'm going to kill your heir."

To some people, this dream seems unreal, and some may say this means nothing. But because my son has been a prophetic dreamer all of his life, I knew that God was saying something to him and me in this dream.

The interpretation to dream is;

The hill top is a place of greater insight, it's where you can see from a great distance. God is revealing a part of the enemy's plan. The plant's hand is an imitation of the Lord. John 15:1 reads, "I am the true vine, and My Father is the vinedresser. Every branch in Me that does not bear fruit, He takes away; and every branch that bears fruit, He prunes it so that it may bear more fruit." This plant that has a vine coming out of it, is a false Christ. It is imitating who Christ Jesus is. The woman is Jezebel. Black represents the mysteries of God here. The rock was black instead of being white, which would have represented Jesus Christ.

So, this dream is speaking of a false Christ, false prophet, and false Holy Spirit scenario. This dream will reveal Jezebel merging with the false Christ-like a symbol then reaching out to people stating "This is the way of God; I am the vine and you are the branches." The whole purpose is to kill everything it touches. The heirs of the vine will be all of the ministries that are attached to this one huge ministry.

The time has come where there are some large ministries in the Earth that seems as if they are attached to Jesus's vine but they are not. We will see from a long way off that there is a Jezebel spirit that has entered into it. Smaller churches that have sprung out from the larger ministries will start dying, and that's the whole point.

The rock is revealing to us that Jezebel is trying to imitate the Father, Son and Holy Spirit because she is a false prophet. Jezebel represents one who is obsessive and controlling, especially in the spirit realm. In the Bible, she replaced the altars of God with the altars of Baal. She also had a righteous man stoned to death when he would not sell his land to Ahab the king, her husband.

This Jezebel spirit is about to invade a vast network, that proposes to be Christian, and it's going to bring about the death of it. There will be a fraction of the network that is solid and will try to resist even though they are in the wrong as well.

This is another warning of what is going to happen in the last days, "The One World Religion." The dream is almost spelling it out. Every year there is a meeting held with the Pope, called Conference of Secretaries of Christian World Communion. There is a leader from every religion that is a part of it from the Anglian church to the Pentecostal church and even the Seven Day Adventist church is involved. They are all coming together to promote unity with Babylon. The people who are already involved with this, are singing praises to the Pope for bringing this One World Religion into play. A few of the names that surprised me were, Kenneth Copeland, and Joel Osteen. My heart weeps because John Osteen would have never agreed to this.

The One World Religion is about bringing the World under control of one system. Revelation the 17th chapter talks about there being 2 beasts. One will arise up from the ocean and the other one will arise from the land. The Beast that rises from the ocean will be the Antichrist who is the horrible and cruel leader, and the one arising from the land is the one deceiving the people by pretending he is pointing them to Jesus first. He is already in the Earth working. Once he wins the heart of the people, he will then start to lead them into following the Antichrist. This One World Religion is to just usher the Antichrist into the land. If you study Revelation, you will then see that the Antichrist in the end kills the other beast. Which means he is going to use that leader over that particular religion, and then kill him.

If you ever wondered which religion will one day control all churches here on earth, let me give you my opinion. It is the Catholic Church. Why do I say that? Well who is heading up the Conference of Secretaries of Christian World Communion? Who is bringing all the religions together and discussing the One World Religion? It's the Catholic Church. Besides that, did you know that Catholic means Universal? Universal was meant to be all over the World and to be the Religion for the World. So many religions are declaring that division is coming to an end.

1 Thessalonians 5th chapter and 3rd verse say "While they are saying, Peace and Safety, then destruction will come upon them suddenly." They will claim that peace will come out of this One World Religion but it's only to bring everyone under their control.

On February 17, 2020, I had a dream that one of my spiritual nephews was getting married. When I made it to the house where his fiancé was, she was still getting dressed for the wedding. While I waited for her, I began to hear something rattling under the bed. There was a young man in the room, so I asked him to move the mattress from the bed. When he removed the mattress, I saw that there were 6 rope like fabrics under the bed. The guy said "see, there's nothing under here". I said to him, "no, wait just one second and do not move". After about 3 seconds, one of the rope-like fabrics began moving and it was actually a gray snake with spots all over it. Once that snake moved, the other 5 snakes started moving around. I said to him, "I knew it was a snake under that bed, but I didn't know that there were 6 of them. So, I jumped up and moved quickly out of the way.

The interpretation of this dream almost falls in line with my son's dream. This dream was about a church. My spiritual nephew represents a fake Jesus and his fiancé represents a new Christian, or new babe in Christ. The fake Jesus is an antichrist, and if the baby Christian does not seek to know God by building a relationship with Him, she will be deceived by the antichrist.

Snakes represent lies being told. The color gray means wisdom, while the black spots represents sin in this dream. This reveals that this is the antichrist. God is going to reveal who the antichrist is and show us that he is not a part of the Body of Christ and he is not the Bride of Christ.

The antichrist's intentions are to lead the babes in Christ astray. The true Groom is Christ Jesus, and His Bride is the true church. We must stay aware of what is going on in the World. Saints, we can't continue to be ignorant of satan's devices. Be discerning, God has given us this gift. If you don't have the gift of discernment, ask God for it. We have to discern the times, so we can always be prepared for what is the coming of the Lord.

CHAPTER Eleven

The Great Revival is on its Way

I had a dream that my sister, Deborah was getting married and Pastor Hart Ramsey was the officiating Pastor for the wedding. I remember his wife, Kandis gave me a gorgeous dress to wear to the wedding. The wedding was in this big beautiful grassy field. I was with my 2 spiritual brothers, Pastor James Miller and Prophet Omega George on the day of the wedding. Pastor Kim Burrell was preparing to sing at the wedding.

I remember Deborah was on top of this mountain and Pastor Kim Burrell was now singing. My other 2 younger sisters, Yvonne and Robin were late. They made it to the wedding right before Pastor Kim finished her song. As soon as they showed up, we saw that Pastor Kim had shot Deborah out in the air from a canon and Deborah was in the air inside of this big bubble floating down to the ground to meet her fiancé.

Once that happened, Pastor Kim slid down this water slide with no water on it with her high heels on in this pretty, peach color dress. When she hit the ground, she was running, trying to stop herself because of the speed of coming down that slide. I saw her assistant, Katrina at the bottom of the slide running behind her trying to help break her race. Then my sister, Yvonne asked "why did Deborah come off the mountain like that?" I said, because Pastor Kim wanted to surprise her with a unique wedding gift. Then I woke up.

The interpretation of this dream is; Deborah represents the Bride of Christ, which is not yet present. Pastor Hart Ramsey represents our Father, God. Lady Kandis Ramsey represents Jesus and Pastor Kim Burrell represents the Holy Spirit in this dream. All of them have a personal connection with God.

The Holy Spirit brings the Bride of Christ onto the mountain top of destiny. Pastor Kim, who is operating as the Holy Spirit is launching the Bride of Christ, which is God's plan for the Church. His plans will have all to do with miraculous jobs and operating in the Spirit of God.

The bubble that Deborah as the bride was floating in the air reveals to us that in order to operate in this miraculous place, we need to be cleansed.

Pastor Kim sliding from the mountain top to the ground and then running is the revelation of the flow of the Holy Spirit, and how we have to be ready to run with Him in this hour. He is getting us ready for the coming of the Lord.

My two younger sisters who are late, represents that there will be many people who are a part of the Body of Christ that will be late in getting to the ceremony. The ceremony that the Holy Spirit has planned for the Church. Some will wonder what is happening. Some will come in asking why are things being done like this? Who did that? Who told them to do it that way? They will be concerned about what is happening instead of being concerned about what plans God have for us in this season.

The color peach that Pastor Kim was wearing represents perseverance and persistence in righteousness. After we persevere and have been persistent in righteousness, there will be an outpouring of God's Spirit. A great revival is on the way, and God is going to pour out His Spirit on all of those who are ready to receive it. Will you be ready?

<u>CHAPTER Twelve</u>

The Glory of the Lord is falling

Ezekiel 1:4-5

"And I looked, and, behold, a whirlwind came out of the north, a great cloud, and a fire infolding itself, and a brightness was about it, and out of the midst thereof as the color of amber, out of the midst of the fire. Also, out of the midst thereof came the likeness of four living creatures. And this was their appearance; they had the likeness of a man." (NASB)

Ezekiel 1:28

"As the appearance of the bow that is in the cloud in the day of rain, so was the appearance of the brightness roundabout. This was the appearance of the likeness of the glory of the Lord. And when I saw it, I fell upon my face and I heard a voice of one that spake." (KJV)

On March 11, 2020 my cousin Dewonna had a dream where she was in a car lot looking at cars. There were a lot of people also in this car lot. She saw a man looking at this small, white and blue expensive car. All of a sudden, the Lord appeared in the sky and there were three to four people with Him, and they were gathered in a circle. The colors were absolutely beautiful, just unexplainable. Then a light started to beam from them, like the glare from the Sun.

No one on the car lot saw Jesus or the people who appeared with Him in the sky, only Dewonna. While standing there, she stared and thought to herself, "how beautiful this is". Then sprinkles of gold starting falling from the sky and she ran under it so it could fall on her. She noticed that no one else could see what was happening. The gold sprinkles stopped for a moment, and then it began to fall heavily upon the Earth.

Now this time the others saw the gold sprinkling down and they began to run under the sprinkles and became covered with it. She then began to look to her right and there she saw more people covered in the gold sprinkles and the fire of God was all over them.

She then began to ask the Lord to let that fire fall on her, and it did.

This dream is concerning the Body of Christ. It is about the coming Revival and an outpouring of God's Spirit.

A car lot represents vehicles that control our movement in life. Also, it represents personal ministries. This is revealing the places the Body of Christ is going to become equipped to move forward and quickly in their destinies. It could be a church or a ministry that is helping the body of Christ to prepare for moving forward in their destinies, ministries or life itself. The cars are for sale, and the expensive car that she saw was white and blue represents righteousness, communion with God and revelation from God.

Often, we talk about the gift of Salvation being free, but there is a pearl of great price, and the communion with God and revelation from God is at a high price. We have to be willing to set aside or lay aside everything else to seek Him and Him alone.

We need to let God be the dividing line in our lives, which is quite expensive. The dream is showing there is communion and revelation that is available from God to help us move forward, and toward our destiny, but it does come with a price.

God is expecting us to be Holy as He is Holy, and to separate ourselves from the World and Worldly things. He expects us to leave sin behind because we are the Body of Christ. The people who are at the car lot, are people who are trying to get on the road to their destiny.

The Lord appearing in the sky with the 3-4 people represents Hebrews 12:1 "Therefore, since we are surrounded by so great a cloud of witnesses, let us also lay aside every weight and the sin that clings so closely, and let us run with perseverance the race that is set before us," The

Lord's appearing is going to be clear where all the World can see Him, and that is up in the sky. The sky is a north position that means judgment is here.

He is revealing where He can truly be found, not saying He will show up on Earth, but it's where His Presence will be. That's what the Gold Sprinkles represents, which is God's glory and His Presence. The Lord's appearance coming out of nowhere represent the Glory of God which means the coming of the Messiah.

So, the Lord is announcing, "I'm coming soon, here is my gold or my glory, and you will see My glory falling from where I am. If you don't see My glory falling where you are, then My Presence is not there. If My Presence isn't there then you aren't being equipped for your destiny. You must come where I am, where My Presence is."

We as the Body of Christ must know this, that there are many places for the equipping of our destinies, however, we have to be where the Lord's glory is dwelling. Where His glory is, His fire will fall, which is the Revival and outpouring of the Holy Spirit. (Isaiah 10:16b and under His glory He shall kindle a burning like the burning of a fire) The Lord is saying "Don't be afraid to ask for My fire or for more of Me. I want to give you more of Me. I want you to experience what you haven't experienced in Me. When we get that hunger and thirst for righteousness, then we shall be filled. (Matthew 5:6 KJV)

Can you say that you are ready for the outpouring of the Holy Spirit? Are you looking for the great Revival of God? Are you ready to travel down the road of your destiny? Are you ready for the coming of the Lord? These are questions that must be asked in this season.

CHAPTER Thirteen

The Year of the Mouth

The year 2020 is the year of the MOUTH. It looks like it should mean 20/20 Vision but remember, God's ways and thoughts are not ours. He does not see things like we do. The enemy doesn't want us to declare or decree anything as Prophets are prophetic voices in this hour. God wants the Prophets to sound the alarm and speak His Word aloud. "Don't go silent in this hour, and never stop releasing what I am saying" says the Lord.

Because this is the year of the mouth, what we speak, declare and decree really matter. One of the reasons the pandemic hit us this year is because the enemy wants us to shut our mouths. The mask is to quiet us in this hour concerning the things of God.

All we see now on television is news about the pandemic. This news is to drive us into a state of fear. Because they want us to be afraid, so much of the media has hyped up this COVID19 virus. I am not saying what we are hearing is not true about the COVID19, however, I am saying all that we hear about the virus is not true. There is a reason for the hype and it is control. I once heard someone say, "Behind a global control is always a culture of fear" (unknown author).

The supreme leader of North Korea, Kim Jong Un, went into the office after his father, bringing great fear to the people. Because they feared him, he controlled them with no problem. Oh, but we serve a Mighty and Awesome God. Our Father protects us. Kim Jong Un did not become supreme leader until 2011, but in 2006 Prophet Kim Clement prophesied and said, "North Korea and South Korea will become one again. North Korea, your president is dead. He is already dead. The Lord says, I have already written it, your days are numbered, you have been counted in the balances, therefore Kim, it is now time for you to face this, that you have done as being iniquitous, you are no longer alive, you are a vegetable, and you are brain dead."

"The Lord said because of that, I will bring about a unity between North and South Korea, and a great move of God shall come from there." This was before he ever got into office, God was encouraging His people. God gave this people in North and South Korea a promise. So, with the promises of God, unlimited power is released. We must declare and decree what God says, whether it is from His Word or from a Prophetic Word He speaks through His Prophets.

In 2017, Prophetess Jennifer LeClaire prophesied that North and South Korea would reunite also. I know many may say "She heard Prophet Kim Clement say that", but she spoke on one of her YouTube videos that she never heard him say it. I believe her, because many of us who are prophets, watch very little television or none at all, and so we aren't aware of a lot of things that are going on or what is being said.

At this time, for the past week, we have been hearing that Kim Jong Un is now in a vegetable state, which means, he is brain dead, just like Prophet Kim Clement prophesied. Some had even said on April 26, 2020, is already dead, which was also prophesied by Prophet Kim Clement. At this time, only God knows the truth and Kim Jong Un family.   If he is still alive, then it is only a matter of time before we hear that he has truly past from life to death. God never breaks a promise, and He will never tell a lie.

CHAPTER Fourteen

Do Conspiracy Theories Have Some Truth to It?

I want to introduce here in this chapter some of what people call conspiracy theories. The thing about theories is, there is some truth in them if not all truth. We have to pray to receive the revelation of what is the truth that lies within the theory.

The first theory I want to introduce is with Anthony Patch. There is an interview played on Regan F Peabody YouTube page on March 26, 2020, where Anthony Patch spoke about the Coronavirus on January 14, 2014.

He talked about a man-made virus that was created in the Middle East, it had made its way to Europe, and it was called the Coronavirus which was a Respiratory Disease. Because it was airborne, he said, "it would reach around the World." It is said by Live Science news that the Coronavirus hit the U.S. in January 2020, six years after Patch spoke of it.

Patch believes that the Coronavirus was derived so that a vaccine would be created. He also believes that the disease along with other diseases, have been created by man not only to kill off the human race but to put a demand out for a vaccine. Why would they want people to demand the vaccine? Anthony stated "because there is something in the vaccine, they want people to have in their bodies. "I began to think, what would they want to put in our bodies? The answer that Patch gave was "a DNA Manipulator."

Anthony Patch, began to explain that those who created the virus had created a 3 strand of DNA. It will be transported into a person's body, through a vaccine that the person is demanding to have because of virus or flu. He stated, "the government knows that they can't force us to take the vaccine or a 3 strand of DNA, but if they create the problem, and then present a solution, their ultimate goal will be achieved." That makes a lot of sense to me.

What happens if a person does take the vaccine? Patch states, "almost immediately, their DNA undergoes a transformation. Almost immediately, thy realize they have lost their independence, their ability to think on their own, and to make their own decisions." He also said, "their morals and religious beliefs all go away."

Once you have lost your independence, what happens next was so shocking. He stated, "they can now control you, turn you into a class of slaves to serve the elite. They want to turn us into trans-humanism, where we can live forever without God". If this is so, no one can tell me that Satan isn't behind this. Only God can deliver us from such a mess. But how can God deliver us when our hearts are turned toward the things of the world and away from the things of God?

We are so focused on the democrats and the republicans arguing about a stimulus check, while the elite could be plotting to take away our rights and freedom. If they do that, we won't need any stimulus packages. The coronavirus has nothing to do with politics, this has all to do with control.

I wish I could give all of the information Mr. Patch has spoken concerning this, but I can't. You can go to YouTube or Amazon and look up Anthony Patch for his videos and books and began to do your own research. I have bought one of his books and I plan to buy many more so that I am not deceived by Satan's devices. Please Pray and allow God to reveal all truth to you.

The second theory I want to look at is; The Denver Airport. I believe this shocked me more than anything I had ever heard in my life. This is also found on YouTube. Just pull up conspiracy theories about the Denver Airport and you will see a lot of this information in video. One particular video I looked at was Daily Blast Live.

The Conspiracy Theory of the Denver Airport leaves people with so many questions. One question is, when you see the airport from the skies, why does it look like a Nazi symbol? Why is there a Masonic Capstone at the airport, especially since the Freemasonry is a secret society?

Another conspiracy theory about the airport is, the tunnel. There is said to be 3 floors to the tunnel, but only one floor that was named the 3rd floor was actually said to have been for baggage transporting. So, when asked, where is floor 1 and floor 2? The reply was, "there isn't a 1st and 2nd floor in the tunnel." That really doesn't make sense to me and no one else.

Okay. I really want to talk about what pictures are Muraled on the walls of the airport. The YouTube video "7 Creepy Conspiracy Theories about the Denver airport" is a video that may open your eyes to somethings.

This video gave some facts about the Denver Airport like, the construction of the airport fell 16 months behind schedule, and went $2 Billion over budget, which cost Denver $4.8 Billion to build.

The theories they are mentioning are; one, there is an underground facility meant to act as an emergency bunker for the Global Elite made up of billionaires, world leaders, politicians, and celebrities. Allegedly there is also a vast underground network of New World Order Command Bunkers, and a FEMA concentration camp for future use.

There was a construction worker that claimed that the construction building was delayed because there were 5 multi story buildings that had been built beneath the airport.

What if this is true? This is just me thinking right now. Could it be the plans of the elite are to use the weapon of mass destruction, chemical weapon to try and wipe out most of the World? And all who are left will become the elites slaves in the concentration camp? Hmmmmm

Another conspiracy theory I want to bring out is the theory when you enter the Denver Airport is that there is a horse Mustang Statue that has been named Blucifer which is thought to be cursed.

The name Blucifer has the name Lucifer (satan's name when he was an angel) inside of it, as if he was still an angel. It is also said to be the fourth horse of the Apocalypse. Which Revelation 6:8 talks about, "I looked, and behold, an ashen horse; and he who sat on it had the name Death; and Hades was following with him.

Authority was given to them over a fourth of the earth, to kill with sword and with famine and with pestilence and by the wild beasts of the earth." The one thing I do know is that Satan has no new tricks and he has no creativity. Everything he does is in an attempt to emulate God.

The video continues, and it now speaks on the dedication stone. It has the Freemason Logo on it, he says. The Freemasons is a secret fraternal society that's allegedly the largest in the World. It has existed since the 18th Century and could be even earlier than that. The stone reads that the airport is dedicated on March 19, 1994 which that number represents 33 which is the highest level you can get in Freemasonry. The stone also has written on it "The New World Airport Commission Contributors". The New World Order is thought to be a small group of powerful people secretly working together throughout history to form an all-powerful Global Government.

Now the murals by Leo Tanguma. The theory behind the first mural, which is entitled, peace and harmony in nature, allegedly is to address the destruction of the environment. The second mural is entitled, the children of the world dream of peace. It is supposed to get rid of violence in society. Allegedly these murals are showing how the Illuminati affects life in every way. In this same video, it's said that the Denver Office of Cultural affairs has pubic outlined processes of choosing the artwork for the airport. A project of community members and artist chose the artwork for the airport but it must be approved by several government committees and the Mayor before being commissioned.

The third mural shows 3 dead women from all different nationalities. Would a committee of artists agree for such to be put on a mural painting, 3 dead women?

I really don't believe so. But, if this conspiracy theory has any truth to it, we then, as the Body of Christ really need to pray and fast like never before.

Now I want to talk about a documentary some may call a Conspiracy Theory, but I believe there is some truth to it. The documentary is called "Out of Shadows. (not out of the shadows) The documentary was recorded by people who aren't religious fanatics, but they are people who were deep in Hollywood.

It is a one hour video you can find on YouTube and it is a must to see it. I want to bring out just a few things that I believe will open up your curiosity to why we believe everything we see on television.

Out of the Shadows talks about the entertainment world, which is music, movies, and television. It is showing us how the government has always controlled our content but we have never paid attention to it. The narrator asks, "who is influencing our content?"

I purposely made this the last chapter, because I wanted the Christians to read this chapter out of curiosity so it can help set us free. We as Christians are so far behind time because when information is presented to us, we shut it out and say, that stuff isn't real. Or we may say, well, if it is real, God will take care of it. We love being ignorant, even after God has said to us, "don't be ignorant of satan's devices." Church it is time to open up our eyes to see and ears to hear what God is trying to reveal to us.

If I have never been serious about watching any video in my life, I am so serious about this one. God put this video in my pathway for me to watch, no one else pointed this out to me. I have literally begged others to watch it, all because it changed my life. For days I walked around in a daze asking God, can this be true? I can't tell you a lot about this documentary because I want you to go and watch it so you can get the full story. There are a few things that I would like to bring in from the video, and I am hoping its okay. for me to do.

The narrator is a guy who decided to look into the satanic rituals that go on in Hollywood after his Christian Therapists explained to him that little girls, little boys and ladies are being abused by Satanists and she is having to put their lives back together after it happens. He explained in the documentary how he found out the information and what he saw.

Please go watch the documentary, the title is "Out of Shadows" He explained in the video that he did not find God in the church. He began to believe that God is real because he saw that the Luciferins and the occult world were real and he had been fooled to believe they weren't. He became really scared when he stumbled discovered it for himself.

If a producer in Hollywood, who did not know the Lord but was now aware of the demonic and satanic occultic world does exist, why doesn't the church believe also?

The Word of God has it laid out for us, are we not reading the Bible or maybe we are reading but not really believing it. My heart was broken as I continued to watch the documentary on YouTube, we have wasted a lot of time doing what the World does, but we still call ourselves the Body of Christ.

The video then began to talk about how they believe that the things that are on television and movies are teaching bad morals to our children as well as adults. These movies and games are desensitizing us when it comes to violence and sex. I'll also add that television programs are also desensitizing us to perversion. It makes us think or accept this is now the norm. However, if the Bible says it is an abomination unto God then it will always be an abomination unto God. God is the same yesterday, today and forever. He does not change.

One of the gentlemen in this video talked about how sexual abuse between the ages of 1-6 causes a child to have split personalities and disassociated behaviors.

It talks a little about the church of Satan and when they arrived on the scene in the late 1960s and early 1970s.

The head of that church is Antoine La Vey. Eddie Murphy is shown speaking of how Sammy Davis Jr. was saying he works for the devil and that Satan is as powerful as God. I discover that, Sammy Davis Jr. was actually associated with Antoine La Vey the leader of the satanic church.

Then there is Michael Aquino who was in the U.S. Army, and working in the CIA, a practicing Satanist. It was discovered that he was running a pedophile ring out of one of the government training centers.

Fifty children came out and said he had performed sexual acts on them but he walked away from courts a free man.

The video talked about Jeffery Epstein, who had been arrested for allegedly sex trafficking young girls. It was said that Jeffery had pictures and videos of many Politian's,

Hollywood Celebrities, and Music Artists who were sexually abusing these underaged girls. These acts were being performed on Epstein's planes, and his Island called Orgy Island. Allegedly, many Celebrities and Politicians were being blackmailed because of the videos, and pictures that were taking at the Playboy Mansion.

Liz Crokin has worked as an investigative journalist, columnist and senior editor for various publications for over a decade who began to speak out about this pedophile ring and they declared her out of her mind.

Liz said she was well respected in the media world until she started speaking on Pizzagate.

The Pizzagate was allegedly connected to Hilary Clinton, John Pedesto, and Barak Obama where emails were found connecting them to this pedophile ring. Reality Check News talked about this and showed the emails from each of them. Information was found on Anthony Weiner's computers showing where Hilary Clinton was connected to the Pedophile ring.

In one of the emails it read, "Obama spent $65,000 of the tax payers money flying in the pizza and dogs from Chicago for a private party at the White House not long ago, assume we are using the same channels". Allegedly this is an email that connected Obama to the Pizzagate.

These emails even had symbols that address or pointed out the Pedophiles preference were, whether they wanted a boy or a girl.

Per Reality Check News, Ben Swann reported there were never an investigation performed not from the local police, state police or FBI, no one investigated any of this. My question and I am sure many others are asking, "Why wasn't an investigation performed, especially when it comes to molestation of children?"

It has been said that "Pizzagate" is a conspiracy. Only God knows the truth about this situation.

No one, including John Pedosta can explain the code words that were in the emails. He has not explained why he has children rented for his adult entertainment parties yet, says Liz Crokin. She explains that he also has pedophile cannibalism paintings all over his office and home.

Liz stated, "People who blow the whistle on these pedophiles tend to turn up dead." Jeffrey Epstein was found dead in a jail cell. It was reported by NBC News that he committed suicide. It was said that more than 50 people wanted him dead.

Out of Shadows documentary spoke on Epstein's flight log, which had many popular names in Hollywood, Politics and of great power here on Earth. There were names such as members of the Royal Family, Prince Andrew, Naomi Campbell, and Kevin Spacey. It was shown that Bill Clinton's name was written over 25 times on the list, and Hilary Clinton had been to Epstein's Island.

Allison Mack who was starred in "Smallville", was arrested for an occult sexual case. She was a member of this occult that was trafficking children that were also running preschools in Mexico.

Allegedly, there are Elite pedophile rings that do exist, and they have been funded by wealthy individuals, including Clare Bronfman, Sara Bronfman, and Nancy Saulsmen. These rings were using the preschools to traffic children.

It is explained in the documentary that for the music or Hollywood industry, you aren't allowed to reach a certain level of success unless you are willing to join their club, or be a part of their secret society. Neither will they allow them to obtain a lot of fame or power unless they can control you.

A few examples are Katy Perry who used to be a gospel singer, got into Hollywood and was introduced to the occult world, she's now doing videos of her being in hell, with satanic themes and she is now highly successful. Lady Gaga has always been named among them.

Allegedly, Satanists have to reveal who they are in some way, shape or form. That's why we see occult members in Hollywood, constantly flaunting symbolism. Some of the symbols are the pyramid, the one eye which is shown on many front-page magazines, and then a 666 symbol. Then they have the pedophile symbols which is a swirl logo and the triangle that looks like a pyramid.

Elijah Woods speaks out and says, "Hollywood has a pedophilia problem." There are many people who are in Hollywood, Music Industry and Politics that probably agrees with Elijah Woods because they know the truth. All those in Hollywood, in the Music Industry or in Politics are not all bad but many are, and they have very negative agendas.

We as Christians need to begin to pray and seek the Lord for the children who are wrapped up and tangled up in these pedophile rings. We should pray they are released back to their families. We should also pray about the television programs we watch, the lyrics in the songs we are listening to that are from the secular world. As the church we must stay in the face of God in this season so that we won't be ignorant of Satan's devices, whether through conversation with friends, or through television and radio.

God expects more from us Sisters and Brothers. Are we willing to do whatever it takes to please our Father in this season? God loves us, and second coming of Jesus Christ is close whether the world believes it or not.

Just know that we are in the End Times, use your time wisely. I pray that after reading this book, your eyes and ears will open to see and hear what the Spirit of the Lord is saying to the Church around the World.

Chapter Fifteen

Signs of the second coming of Christ Jesus

One sign of the second coming of Christ is increasing danger of nuclear war. Nuclear weapons if used can destroy all of mankind. Studies have shown that countries that have nuclear weapons are:

1. United States

2. Russia

3. China

4. United Kingdom

5. France

6. Pakistan

7. Israel

8. India

9. North Korea

The United States and Russia has over 5000 nuclear warheads and both were considering to increase their nuclear weapon capability as at 2018.

Revelation 9:16-18 Discusses the Army from the East

The number of the armies of the horsemen was two hundred million; I heard the number of them. And this is how I saw in the vision the horses and those who sat on them: *the riders* had breastplates *the color* of fire and of hyacinth and of brimstone; and the heads of the horses are like the heads of lions; and out of their mouths proceed fire and smoke and brimstone. A third of mankind was killed by these three plagues, by the fire and the smoke and the brimstone which proceeded out of their mouths.

Remember the dream in chapter 4 concerning the military planes I saw. This chapter is confirming the war dream that God gave me. It speaks of 1/3 of the world will die in this war. I recommend you take the time and read the entire book of Revelation. Pray and ask God to reveal to you the meaning of Revelation.

Another sign will be natural disasters, which includes earthquakes. From January 2010 until February 2019 there were many great earthquakes that hit around the World, allegedly killing almost 300,000 people. (Wikipedia) This sign is found in Matthew 24:7-8. Revelation 16:18 speaks about an even greater Earthquake to come.

The next sign you need to look out for is someone stepping out that will be a religious, respected figure who will influence the political and military powers. This is found in Revelation 17:11-14, The beast which was and is not, is himself also an eighth and is *one* of the seven, and he goes to destruction.

The ten horns which you saw are ten kings who have not yet received a kingdom, but they receive authority as kings with the beast for one hour. These have one purpose, and they give their power and authority to the beast. These will wage war against the Lamb, and the Lamb will overcome them because He is Lord of lords and King of kings, and those who are with Him *are the* called and chosen and faithful."

Then we see in Revelation 13:11-14 which reads, "Then I saw another beast coming up out of the earth; and he had two horns like a lamb and he spoke as a dragon. He exercises all the authority of the first beast in his presence. And he makes the earth and those who dwell in it to worship the first beast, whose fatal wound was healed. He performs great signs so that he even makes fire come down out of heaven to the earth in the presence of men. And he deceives those who dwell on the earth because of the signs which it was given him to perform in the presence of the beast, telling those who dwell on the earth to make an image to the beast who *had the wound of the sword and has come to life."

We know that the King of kings, Lord of lords, the Lamb the beast came against is our Savior, Jesus Christ. The scripture says He will overcome them because of who He is.

Then it talks about there is a second beast that will come out of the earth with two horns like a lamb. We must know that this is the Anti-Christ because he strives to be like God in everything he does.

He will appear to be a Christian but he will speak like a dragon the Bible says. He will also deceive billions of people because they are looking at the signs he will perform, which are false miracles and signs. Matthew 16:4 reads "A wicked and adulterous generation seeketh after a **sign**; and there shall **no sign** be given unto it, but the **sign** of the prophet Jonas. And he left them, and departed."

Because this generation is always looking for signs, the anti-Christ will use signs to deceive many. The Bible is warning us that we should be listening to what is coming out of the mouth of this dragon, not what signs it looks like he is performing.

Another sign will come which is similar to what we all are looking for and that's the great revival. However, this will not be the Great Revival that God is calling us to, but this will be another sign of the anti-Christ. 2 Thessalonians 2:8-12 reads, "Then that lawless one will be revealed whom the Lord will slay with the breath of His mouth and bring to an end by the appearance of His coming; *that is*, the one whose coming is in accord with the activity of Satan, with all power and signs and false wonders, and with all the deception of wickedness for those who perish, because they did not receive the love of the truth to be saved. For this reason, God will send upon them a deluding influence so that they will believe what is false, in order that they all may be judged who did not believe the truth but took pleasure in wickedness."

Then in Matthew 24:15 "Therefore when you see the ABOMINATION OF DESOLATION which was spoken of through Daniel the prophet, standing in the holy place (let the reader understand), then those who are in Judea must flee to the mountains. Whoever is on the housetop must not go down to get the things out that are in his house. Whoever is in the field must not turn back to get his cloak."

This is the sign of the three and half years of tribulation. Daniel is warning us that when this time comes, we will need to flee. He is telling us not to go back to get anything, leave it all behind. The false prophet and false Christ will claim to be Jesus Christ and will try to convince all mankind the he is the Christ. The Bible is telling us not to believe him. Matthew 24:25-27 tells us, Behold, I have told you in advance. So if they say to you, 'Behold, He is in the wilderness,' do not go out, *or*, 'Behold, He is in the inner rooms,' do not believe *them*. For just as the lightning comes from the east and flashes even to the west, so will the coming of the Son of Man be.

The scriptures are telling us that when Jesus returns, He won't have to tell us who He is, we will know without a doubt who He is.

When you hear that the sacrifice of animals are being halted in Israel by the religious Jews, then know that we are in the last days according to Daniel.

Another sign is found in Matthew 24:14 and it reads, "This **gospel** of the kingdom shall be **preached** in the whole world as a testimony **to all** the **nations**, and then the end will come."

When we see that the gospel has reached every nation, then we know we are truly at the end of time. These are just some of the signs God has given us to watch out for. There are so many more and they are found in Daniel, Matthew, and Revelation. I encourage you to pick up your Bible and read it. Don't let the end time catch you still in your sins.

Saints please use this time to be sure that you are ready for the second coming of our Lord, and Savior, Jesus Christ. Pray for your family members and all of those that are connected to you.

God Bless all who take heed to His warnings.